Rome in a Weekend with Two Kids

A Step-By-Step Travel Guide About What to See and Where to Eat
(Amazing Family-Friendly Things to do in Rome When You Have Little Time)

By

Hassan Osman

Rome in a Weekend with Two Kids: A Step-By-Step Travel Guide About What to See and Where to Eat (Amazing Family-Friendly Things to do in Rome When You Have Little Time)
Copyright © 2017 by Hassan Osman.

Notice of Rights
All rights reserved. No part of this publication may be reproduced, distributed, or transmitted in any form or by any means without the prior written permission of the author. Reproduction or translation of this work in any form beyond that permitted by section 107 or 108 of the 1976 United States Copyright Act is strictly prohibited. For permission requests, please contact the author. Reviewers may quote brief passages in reviews.

Liability Disclaimer and FTC Notice
The purpose of this book is to provide the user with general information about the subject matter presented. This book is for entertainment purposes only. This book is not intended, nor should the user consider it, to be legal advice for a specific situation. The author, company, and publisher make no representations or warranties with respect to the accuracy, fitness, completeness, or applicability of the

contents of this book. They disclaim any merchantability, fitness warranties, whether expressed or implied. The author, company, and publisher shall in no event be held liable for any loss or other damages, including but not limited to special, incidental, consequential, or other damages. This disclaimer applies to any damages by any failure of performance, error, omission, interruption, deletion, defect, delay in operation or transmission, computer malware, communication line failure, theft or destruction or unauthorized access to, or use of record, whether for breach of contract, tort, negligence, or under any other cause of action.

By reading this book, you agree that the use of it is entirely at your own risk and that you are solely responsible for your use of the contents. The advice of a competent legal counsel (or any other professional) should be sought. The author, company, and publisher do not warrant the performance, effectiveness or applicability of any sites or references listed in this book. Some links are affiliate links. This means that if you decide to make a purchase after clicking on some links, the author will make a commission. All references and links are for information purposes only and are not warranted for content, accuracy, or any other implied or explicit purpose.

Table of Contents

Introduction 5

Why Read This Book? 6

Your Free Bonus 10

Three Things to Do Before Your Trip 11

How I Planned the Weekend 18

Friday Afternoon 22

Saturday Morning 29

Saturday Afternoon 37

Sunday Morning 45

Sunday Afternoon 52

Conclusion 55

Thank You! 57

Would you like to write a book like this one? 58

Introduction

Rome can be boring for kids.

But it doesn't have to be.

Last summer, I spent a weekend in Rome with my wife and two little girls (aged seven and three), and the trip turned out to be one of the best vacations we have ever had.

We arrived in Italy from the United States on a Friday afternoon, and we left the following Monday morning. So we spent half of Friday and all of Saturday and Sunday in the city.

This book is a short guide that will help you plan your own trip. You get a step-by-step weekend itinerary with pointers about what to do and where to eat. You'll also get food recommendations and must-see highlights to make it a blast for you and your kids.

Why Read This Book?

I'm not an expert on travel, and I'm definitely not an expert on Rome.

In fact, I've never written so much as a blog post about traveling, and I've only been to Rome for a total of two and a half days in my entire life.

So why read a book written by a novice like me?

Here are three reasons why:

1) It's a short book

I like to write books that I personally enjoy reading: short, concise, and no fluff. When I was researching information about visiting Rome with kids, I didn't find what I was looking for. Most books were either too long or too detailed. I didn't have the time to read 300-plus pages about every single tourist destination. I also didn't have the time to read about Rome's ancient history. All I cared about was whether something would be worth my entire family's time and whether we could fit that into our short trip. Because I didn't find a book that met my needs, I wrote this one.

2) It's thoroughly researched and planned

My day job is a project management office manager at Cisco Systems (lawyer-required note: views expressed in this guide are my own). In other words, I plan *everything*. When I was preparing for my trip, I read hundreds of online reviews and blog posts about things to do. I also read a few books about traveling in Rome with children, and I asked friends and colleagues what they personally enjoyed while on their trips. I then cross-checked all those recommendations to balance the must-see highlights with the family-friendly destinations. The end product of all that analysis is in this book.

3) It helps with avoiding FOMO and FOBO

FOMO stands for "Fear of Missing Out" and FOBO stands for "Fear of Better Options." FOMO and FOBO are your enemies during travel because they add unwanted stress.

With only a few days, you will undoubtedly feel like you're going to miss out on something that wasn't part of your plan. This book will help you minimize both FOMO and FOBO because the research has been done on your behalf.

Some caveats

Here are a few things I'd like to point out before you continue reading:

- **This is NOT an extensive travel guide**. This book is not meant to cover everything you can possibly do in Rome. It is designed to solve a specific problem for parents who have limited time to plan for their trip. This means that a lot of activities and landmarks have been intentionally left out. For example, the Vatican is not listed anywhere in the itinerary because every review I read stated that it's not the most family-friendly destination due to long wait lines and very little entertainment value for kids.

- **You can do everything in two full days**. This step-by-step guide is designed for a full weekend, starting on a Friday afternoon and continuing through Sunday evening (i.e., two a half days). However, I built the pla to be flexible enough that it can be completed in just two days if you have to (e.g., Saturday morning through Sunday evening). That's because I have intentionally included an extra half a day as a backup.

- **The activities are gender-neutral**. I have two little girls, and I planned my trip with them in mind. However, the activities are gender-neutral and work for both boys and girls. The activities also work if you have more than two kids.

- **The itinerary is summer-specific**. We visited Rome in late June, so the itinerary focuses on summer activities. Although most of the same landmarks and restaurants could be visited during winter as well, keep in mind that things like public parks or piazzas might less exciting during the colder months.

With that, let's get started with your trip!

Three Things to Do Before Your Trip

Here are three things that I recommend you do before your trip:

1) Download these free phone applications (iPhone or Android)

Google Maps – This was my go-to phone application that I used most of the time in Rome. Google Maps is the best GPS navigation app that gives you addresses for all your landmarks, and shows you the shortest path to walk from one place to another. It also highlights where you are if you're ever lost. Another advantage of Google Maps is that it helps make sure taxis don't take advantage of you by intentionally lengthening the trip (to squeeze more Euros out of you). Whenever we got into a cab, I simply pointed at the path to show the driver that I was aware of how to get to our destination.

TripAdvisor – This application gives you user-generated reviews and pictures of restaurants and things to do in Rome. It uses your location to send you personalized recommendations of nearby places based on input by other travelers. For example, if one of your kids is a picky eater and you need to find a nearby fast-food restaurant, TripAdvisor can show you if there's a McDonald's or Burger King close by. We also used it whenever we wanted to read about famous historic sites that were around us.

Google Translate – This app was a lifesaver. It translates text for over 100 languages, and the Italian to English translation is seamless. It can even translate conversations *on the fly* while you and a foreign language speaker are talking into the app. The most impressive feature, however, is the instant camera translation. You simply point the camera at an Italian phrase on a sign or pamphlet, and it instantly translates the text for you by adding a live-text layer on top. This feature was so jaw-dropping for our kids that it doubled as entertainment for them when we were at restaurants looking over the Italian menus.

Make sure you download all these apps ahead of time and familiarize yourself with their features *before* you get to Rome. The last thing you want to do is waste valuable time figuring out how to use them *while* you're in Rome.

Also, note that these apps require access to the Internet to work, so sign up for an international data plan before you go, or purchase a local mobile phone data plan when you arrive.

2) Buy the following essentials

I won't get into a laundry list of things to buy for your trip, but here are a few items that were extremely helpful for us when we got there:

Water bottles for the kids – Water is free in Rome, and the kids will love drinking directly from the fountains. Bring along a couple of water bottles to fill from the spring fountains and keep your kids hydrated during the long walks. The best bottles we found were the CamelBak Kids' eddy 0.4L water bottles.

Travel ID bracelets – It takes a split second for you to lose sight of your kids in touristy places. Buy a few disposable travel ID bracelets that the children can wear around their wrists or ankles in case they go missing. You can write down the name of your hotel, phone number, and any other information for law enforcement to contact you.

Hats & comfortable shoes – You'll be doing a lot of walking in Rome. Dress appropriately by wearing breathable hats and comfortable walking shoes, especially in mid-summer when the weather gets quite warm.

Portable battery pack – If you're going to use your smartphone for navigation and for photos, you'll definitely drain your battery throughout the day. A portable battery pack will let you charge your phone (and other devices) on the go and avoid wasting time waiting for it to recharge.

International chargers/travel adapters (110V vs 220V) – If you live in the U.S., then your electronic jacks will not fit into the European ones, so you'll need an adapter to be compatible. Also, if your device isn't dual-voltage ready (accepts 110V and 220V), then you'll also need a transformer.

Backpack & small number lock – Everyone warns of pickpockets in Rome who can snatch your wallet or phone in an instant. We carried a backpack and kept all our money and valuables tucked safely inside with a number lock on the zipper. Although unlocking and locking the backpack made it a bit of a hassle every time we needed to pay for something, it was much better than having to check our pockets every two minutes to make sure we didn't get robbed. Get a backpack that has pouches on the sides to carry your kids' water bottles.

Stroller – Although Rome isn't very stroller-friendly because of all the cobblestone and hilly streets, we found it helpful to take ours with us. The kids took turns whenever one of them needed a break. And when they were both tired, one of them sat on the other's lap as we pushed them both along.

Travel credit card & Euros – To avoid foreign transaction fees, sign up for a credit card that waives them for you. A couple that I've used are the Barclaycard Arrival Plus Card and Chase Sapphire Preferred Card. Another good idea is to purchase Euros before your trip (your local bank can provide this service). Although it's usually cheaper to purchase Euros after you land in Rome, having a couple hundred Euros in your pocket before you arrive is definitely a good idea—especially for the cab from the airport.

3) *Get your kids excited about the trip*

The final thing you should do before your trip is to get your kids excited about it early on so that they're passionately looking forward to it.

You can do that by sharing with them what you're going to do and see ahead of time.

For example, show them images of the Pantheon or Piazza Navona using Google's image search. Or use Wikipedia to share interesting tidbits about the landmarks you'll see.

One thing I learned from reading through articles was that the letters *SPQR* (which stand for *Senatus Populusque Romanus*) were used to refer to the Roman people and senate of the ancient Roman Republic. These letters are engraved everywhere on the streets, walls, and monuments. Today, they're even inscribed on taxis. Sharing this fact with my kids ahead of time turned some of our walks into a treasure hunt where they constantly searched for those letters, which helped keep their energy levels up.

For young readers, you can even purchase

an age-appropriate travel book that they can read themselves. *Kids' Travel Guide – Italy & Rome* was one that my seven-year-old particularly enjoyed.

Any investment in time to get them excited early on will definitely pay off later during your visit.

How I Planned the Weekend

Here's the strategy I followed to plan the weekend. You can skip this chapter if you want to, but I wanted to share my approach so that you get an idea of how to go about planning your own weekend if you'd like to make any changes.

First, I read a few books, and hundreds of reviews and blog posts, about places in Rome that were kid friendly.

I then separated the "must-see" landmarks from the "nice-to-see" ones based on personal preference and how family friendly they were. I also researched fun things to do (like tours or activities) and places to eat.

My approach to separating these two lists was simple. I wanted to do things that were authentic to Italy and Rome. When I came across things like the Trevi Fountain (the most gorgeous fountain in all of Europe) or Giolitti (the #1 ranked gelato shop in Rome), those went on the "must-see" list because there was no way we could experience them anywhere else.

However, when I came across things like the

Bioparco (Rome's main zoo) or Knick Knack Yoda (a restaurant known for its tasty hamburgers), those went on the "nice-to-see" list because we could visit a zoo anywhere in the world, and eat awesome burgers back in the U.S. These attractions would serve as back-up destinations in case our primary plan failed or we needed to take a detour.

After that, I started plotting "must-see" landmarks and activities on a map and grouping them in zones to make our itinerary as efficient as possible. I also included places to eat and *gelaterias* (gelato shops) along those paths.

As an ice cream-loving family, one fun decision we made was that we were going to eat gelato every single day—once after lunch, and again after dinner. I researched some of the best gelaterias in town and wanted to be sure we tried as many different places as we could.

Based on all of that, I ended up with four zones:

- **Zone 1**: Trevi Fountain, the Spanish Steps, and Piazza di Spagna
- **Zone 2**: Campo de' Fiori, Piazza Navona, and the Pantheon
- **Zone 3**: Villa Borghese, Pincio

Gardens, and Piazza del Popolo
- **Zone 4**: The Colosseum, Roman Forum, Palatine Hill, and Trastevere

Each zone includes "must-see" landmarks and activities that are within walking distance of each other and can be visited within half a day.

So on Friday afternoon, we did Zone 1. On Saturday, we did Zone 2 in the morning and Zone 3 in the afternoon. Then on Sunday morning, we did Zone 4.

We left Sunday afternoon as a backup for unforeseen events, like getting hit with bad weather one day or waking up late on another.

In between zones, we took a break from the walking and the heat to go back to our hotel and relax. We stayed at the Westin Excelsior Rome Hotel (address: *Via Vittorio Veneto, 125, 00187 Rome, Italy*), which is close to Zones 1 and 3.

For transportation, we went in and out of the zones by cab because that was the most convenient for us as a family. We could have taken the bus and saved some money; a cab ride cost us around €12.00 each way, whereas a bus ride would have cost us €3.00 each way (€1.50 per adult; children under 10 are free). However, we didn't want to go through the hassle of figuring out bus stop transfer times. Moreover, a cab was easier because we had a stroller with us that we plopped in the car trunk instead of hauling it on and off buses.

In the next five chapters, I cover exactly what we did during each half-day.

Friday Afternoon

Spend your Friday afternoon in Zone 1, which includes the Trevi Fountain and Piazza di Espagna. You'll get a great first impression of the city, and taste some amazing gelato. We left the hotel at around 4:00 p.m. and returned around 9:00 p.m., so we spent a good five hours in this zone.

Trevi Fountain

What is it? Famous fountain landmark
Address: *Piazza di Trevi, 00187 Rome, Italy*
Hours: Mon–Sun, 24 hours a day
Admission: Free
Recommended Duration: About 1 hour

Start at one of the most iconic and gorgeous fountains in the world. The Trevi Fountain can get crowded, but it's an absolute must-see. Walk your way down to the edge where the kids will love throwing in coins.

Here are some fun facts to share with your kids: the custom is to turn your back to the fountain and use your right hand to throw a coin over your left shoulder. If you throw in one coin, superstition says you'll return to

Rome someday. If you throw a second, you'll fall in love. If you throw in a third, you'll get married soon.

You can throw in any type of currency; it all goes to a charity that feeds the poor. The fountain collects around $1.5 million U.S. dollars every year, so throwing in coins contributes to a good cause. Just make sure you warn your kids not to step into the water, because you'll get yelled at *and* fined €240.00 by the municipal police officers.

Bartolucci

What is it? Specialty wooden toy shop
Address: *Via dei Pastini, 96-98-99, 00186 Rome, Italy*
Hours: Mon–Sun, 10:00 a.m.–10:00 p.m.
Admission: Free (toy prices vary)
Recommended Duration: About 20 minutes

After Trevi Fountain, walk west on Via delle Muratte which then becomes Via di Pietra ("via" means street in Italian). Walk for five minutes until you reach a hidden wooden toy shop on the left called Bartolucci. This is a shop that sells gorgeous handmade wooden toys. Bartolucci is famous for its Pinocchio models, so you'll get to see a lot of this long-nosed character sprinkled around.

If you want to buy a unique souvenir to impress someone back home, this is the place to get it. The shop is tiny, but we loved it because we got an artisan shop with an authentic feel in the middle of the city.

Giolitti

What is it? Best gelateria in town!
Address: *Via degli Uffici del Vicario, 40, 00186 Rome, Italy*
Hours: Mon–Sun, 7:00 a.m.–2:00 a.m.
Price: €2.50/€4.50 for small/large (cone or cup)
Recommended Duration: About 30 minutes

After Bartolucci, walk north on Via della Guglia for a couple of minutes until you reach a small square called Piazza di Monte Citorio. Turn left onto Via degli Uffici del Vicario, and walk for half a block where you'll see Giolitti on your left. This is a sought-after gelateria in Rome, and it does get pretty busy.

There's also a huge range of flavors. Try the Straciatella, which is a popular flavor in Rome that is similar to chocolate chip ice cream in the U.S., but made with chocolate shavings instead of chocolate morsels.

Spanish Steps

What is it? Famous landmark
Address: *Piazza di Spagna, 00187 Rome, Italy*
Hours: Mon–Sun, 24 hours a day
Admission: Free
Recommended Duration: About 30 minutes

From Giolitti, walk for around 10 minutes to reach the Spanish Steps. There are a few points of interest along the way. As you walk east, passing by the Piazza di Monte Citorio again, you'll come across the Piazza Colonna, where you'll see the beautifully sculpted Marcus Aurelius column. Make a left on Via del Corso, and keep walking north for a few minutes. You'll pass by a cool Disney store on your right if you'd like to make a pit stop there (address: *Via del Corso, 165, 00186 Rome, Italy*).

Then walk east on Via dei Condotti until you reach the Spanish Steps staring down on you at the end of the street. The Spanish Steps is a monumental stairway of 135 steps that was built in the early 1700s. Honestly, there's nothing too earth-shattering about this landmark, but you can have fun with the kids by racing to the top and enjoying the view from the vantage point next to the Obelisco Salustiano, one of five obelisks that were manufactured in Egypt during the Roman period. Then walk back down and ask your kids to sit somewhere on the steps while you take a picture of the crowded stairway from the bottom. You can play "Where's Waldo?" afterward when you look at the pictures.

Piazza di Spagna

What is it? Famous square/historic walking area
Address: *Piazza di Spagna, 00187 Rome, Italy*
Hours: Mon–Sun, 24 hours a day
Admission: Free
Recommended Duration: About 2 hours

At the bottom of the Spanish Steps is the Piazza di Spagna, an iconic square where kids can enjoy running around. Start right at the foot of the steps at the Fontana della Barcaccia, which is a small fountain that means "Fountain of the Ugly Boat." It's designed to look like a half-sunken boat. On its side is a little pedestal that kids can walk on to fill their sippy cups or bottles from water flowing out of the boat's bow.

Spend the afternoon relaxing and strolling around the piazza. In the south part of the piazza is the gorgeous Column of the

Immaculate Conception that depicts the Virgin Mary at the top with four magnificent biblical statues at the base. There are also street shows (live music, acrobatics, etc.) that start early in the evening and are a lot of fun for the kids. The piazza is also famous for its nearby high-end shopping district. Most of the luxury designer brands—including Chanel, Dior, Gucci, Prada, and Fendi—have stores in that zone, so this would be a good time for one parent to get some alone time while the other stays with the kids.

For dinner, try Pastificio Guerra, a nearby Italian fast food shop that serves excellent fresh pasta (address: *Via della Croce, 8, 00187 Rome, Italy*). You can get authentic and inexpensive food in plastic boxes to eat on-the-go, and it's delicious. They serve two selections of pastas that change every day, so choose both flavors and share with your family (price: around €4.00 per pasta dish).

If you're interested in more of a gourmet-type setting, check out Il Gabriello (address: *Via Vittoria, 51, 00187 Rome, Italy*), which is a highly rated restaurant located a few blocks from the piazza (price: around €17.00 per pasta entrée). It's recommended for its lamb chops and fresh seafood. This is a more formal restaurant, so you will need to be dressed appropriately (no shorts allowed).

If your kids are more into fast food, there's also a McDonald's in the southeast corner of the piazza that has free tablet screens at each table to keep children entertained.

Finally, wrap up your evening by trying some heavenly dessert from Pompi Il Regno del Tiramisu (address: *Via della Croce, 82, 00187 Rome, Italy*). They serve the best tiramisu in the city, and it comes in a variety of flavors including classic, chocolate, pistachio, and banana. Their most popular flavor seems to be the strawberry, so try that out first (price: €4.00 per tiramisu piece).

Saturday Morning

Spend your Saturday morning in Zone 2, which includes the area around Piazza Navona and the Pantheon. We left the hotel at around 8:30 a.m. and returned around 1:30 p.m., so we spent about five hours in this zone.

Campo de' Fiori

What is it? Public square/open air market
Address: *Piazza Campo de' Fiori, 00186 Rome, Italy*
Hours: Mon–Sat, 7:00 a.m.–2:00 p.m. (closed on Sundays)
Admission: Free
Recommended Duration: About 1 hour

Start your Saturday morning at Campo de' Fiori, a quaint outdoor market that sells everything from fresh produce to spices. Simply walking around this place gives you a genuine Italian vibe, and several vendors give out free samples for you to try. There are also a couple of stalls selling authentic Italian cheese and honey that are worth checking out.

For a fun experience, have your kids choose some fresh apples from one of the fruit vendors, and wash them in the local drinking fountain before munching on them as a healthy breakfast (price: €1.00 for two apples). My two girls absolutely loved this because it was magical for them to buy and eat their fruit on the spot.

In one corner of the market is Forno Campo de' Fiori, a bakery that is famous for its delicious fresh bread. Stop by to pick up a loaf and share with your family as you continue to stroll around.

Piazza Navona

What is it? Famous public square/historic walking area
Address: *Piazza Navona, 00186 Rome, Italy*
Hours: Mon–Sun, 24 hours a day
Admission: Free
Recommended Duration: About 1 to 2 hours

After Campo de' Fiori, head toward Piazza Navona, which is only an eight-minute walk away.

Start by walking northwest onto Piazza della Cancelleria, then turn left on Corso Vittorio Emanuele II, and right onto Via dei Leutari.

Make a right to get to Piazza di Pasquino. This is a tiny square that's famous for its Pasquino statue. Your kids will enjoy learning about Rome's first "talking statue," where people posted anonymous notes around its neck to complain about religious or civil authorities. Today, you can still see posted complaints on a bulletin board right next to the statue. (To help preserve it, they've stopped allowing the public to hang anything on the statue itself.)

After the statue, continue east onto Via di Pasquino and you'll reach Piazza Navona, one of the most famous and highly popular piazzas in Rome.

The piazza is a long rectangular public square that has three fountains that your kids can also throw coins into. The most popular fountain is the one in the middle, called Fontana dei Quattro Fiumi (fountain of the four rivers), which represents the four main rivers of the world: the Nile, the Danube, the Ganges, and the Río de la Plata. Make a game out of it by having your kids guess which river is which.

Hang around the piazza for an hour or two and enjoy some of the street shows. If it gets too hot, you can walk into the Chiesa di Sant'Agnese in Agone, a 17th century Baroque church that houses great paintings and sculptures (entrance is free).

The Pantheon

What is it? Famous landmark/Roman temple
Address: *Piazza della Rotonda, 00186 Rome, Italy*
Hours: Mon–Sat, 8:30 a.m.–7:30 p.m. | Sun, 9:00 a.m.–6:00 p.m.
Admission: Free
Recommended Duration: About 30 minutes

The Pantheon is only a five-minute walk from Piazza Navona. To get there, start by heading north on Via Agonale, then turn right on Piazza delle Cinque Lune, and make another right at the end of the street. Then turn left on Via di S. Giovanna d'Arco, and continue straight until you reach the intersection, where you'll see a well-known toy shop called Città del sole in the corner (address: *Via della Scrofa, 65, 00186 Rome, Italy*). This is worth a quick visit with your kids because they sell creative and educational toys.

Then continue onto Via del Pozzo delle Cornacchie, and make a right onto Via della Rosetta, a narrow street that leads to the Pantheon at the far end of it.

The Pantheon is a magnificent piece of architecture that served as a Roman temple when it was built 2000 years ago. There can be long lines to get in, but they move pretty quickly.

The best part about the Pantheon is its dome, which is the largest unreinforced solid concrete dome in the world to this day. When you walk in, make your way to the middle and look up at the center of the dome's ceiling to see an opening to the sky called an "oculus," which is just awe-inspiring to watch.

Spend some time inside walking along the edges and looking at the artifacts, making sure you keep your voice down because the Pantheon is considered a place of worship. The Pantheon is not very large, so the entire visit can be really quick. We were in and out in around twenty minutes.

After you leave, try a phenomenal pre-lunch cup of coffee at the nearby La Casa del Caffe Tazza d Oro (address: *Via Degli Orfani 84, 00186 Rome, Italy*), which also sells high quality coffee presses if you're a serious coffee drinker (price: €2.10 per espresso).

Ristorante Al Braciere

What is it? Italian restaurant (optional private pizza-making class)
Address: *Via della Chiesa Nuova 12/13, 00186 Rome, Italy*
Hours: Mon–Fri, 11:00 a.m.–11:00 p.m. | Sat–Sun, 11:00 a.m.–12:00 a.m.
Price: Around €8.00 for a medium pizza; €200.00+ for a pizza class for four (food & drinks included)
Recommended Duration: About 1.5 hours

After visiting the Pantheon, have lunch at Ristorante Al Braciere, a restaurant that lets you make your own pizza. To get there, you'll have to walk around 15 minutes back west toward the far side of Piazza Navona (I'll spare you the step-by-step directions; simply plop the address into Google Maps and it'll show you the shortest path).

This restaurant is an awesome experience where you'll learn how to make authentic-style Italian pizzas with your entire family. The class is a bit pricey but totally worth it. To this day, when I ask my kids what they loved most about our trip, they respond with, "Making pizza."

To start, we all put on our special aprons, which we wore as we worked through the entire process. The chef taught the kids how to make the dough from scratch and roll it out. He then showed them how to put the toppings and helped them slide the pizzas into the oven. We then got to eat our custom-made pizzas, which were some of the best thin-crust pizzas we've ever had.

If you're interested in the class, you'll have to sign up in advance because the slots fill up really fast. The restaurant takes reservations through a third party site called Rome4KidsTours.com, which was great to work with. They also offer pasta-making classes if you're more interested in that. Use the coupon code **"Discount4you"** when booking any of their services to get a special 5% discount.

Here's the direct link to the pizza-making class we signed up for:

https://rome4kidstours.com/pizza-master-class/

If you decide not to sign up for classes, Al Braciere is still an excellent spot to have a regular à la carte lunch. They have some solid reviews about their homemade ravioli and bruschetta.

La Gelateria Frigidarium

What is it? Gelateria
Address: *Via del Governo Vecchio, 112, 00186 Rome, Italy*
Hours: Mon–Sun, 10:30 a.m.–1:00 a.m.
Price: €2.00/€4.00 for small/large (cone or cup)
Recommended Duration: About 1.5 hours

After lunch, grab a scoop of gelato at Frigidarium, a nearby gelateria that's a couple minutes away from the restaurant. Head north on Via della Chiesa Nuova and then make a right onto Via del Governo Vecchio. You'll see Frigidarium on the right.

Try a scoop of your favorite flavor dipped in their heavenly melted dark chocolate, which is a specialty of theirs.

Then head over to your hotel to rest a bit before the midday sun hits. We found it very refreshing to return to the air-conditioned hotel room so that the kids could take a short nap or rest their tired feet. We also used that time to catch up on email and connect with family back home.

Saturday Afternoon

After your break, spend your Saturday afternoon and evening in Zone 3, which includes the area around Villa Borghese and Piazza del Popolo. We left the hotel at around 3:30 p.m. and returned later in the evening at around 9:00 p.m., so we spent approximately five and a half hours in Zone 3.

Villa Borghese

What is it? Rome's main park
Address: *Pizzale del Museo Borghese, 00155 Rome, Italy*
Hours: Mon–Sun, dawn till dusk
Admission: Free (activity prices listed below)
Recommended Duration: About 2 to 3 hours

Villa Borghese is a huge and gorgeous park that feels like an oasis in the middle of Rome. This is one spot you don't want to miss. There's so much to do that you can literally spend your entire afternoon here and not feel guilty about it.

Start by renting a 4-person, 4-wheel bike, which lets you strap your kids in the front while you paddle on next to your partner in the back (there are also 6-person bikes if you have a larger family).

The remarkable thing about these bikes is that they're semi-motorized, which means they help assist you in biking up the hilly paths of the park. This made the ride a much more pleasurable experience because we didn't expend a lot of energy pedaling while we enjoyed the panoramic garden views. The bikes cost around €12.00 to €20.00 for an hour (for the whole family). You'll need to leave your ID—a passport or country-issued ID—to rent one.

A different section of the park also rents out regular bikes or manual single-seater go-karts (€4.00–€8.00 per person, per hour) if you prefer to drive around separately.

After the bike ride, head over to the Casina di Raffaello, a library full of toys located in the middle of the park. This playhouse is dedicated to children aged three to ten. For a €7.00 fee per child, kids get access to some fun activities and educational workshops. There is also an outdoor area with wooden structures where they can play around. The building also houses the main public bathrooms in the park if you need them. The library closes at 7:00 p.m. on the weekends, and 6:00 p.m. on most weekdays (see *http://www.casinadiraffaello.it* for more details on hours).

Within the park, there's also the Bioparco, Rome's main zoo. This can be worth visiting with your kids, but keep in mind that you'll easily spend a few hours here if you want to see all the exhibits. The zoo is huge, and the visit will take up all of your afternoon. We skipped going because our kids regularly get to see zoos and farms back home, and because the Bioparco wasn't rated very highly based on the majority of online reviews. Tickets are €16.00 for adults and €13.00 for children between the ages of one and ten. The zoo opens at 9:30 a.m. daily, and closes between 5:00 p.m. and 7:00 p.m., depending on the season (see *http://www.bioparco.it* for more details).

Nearby is a stunning little lake where you can rent a rowboat and absorb the picturesque scenery from the water. Kids will have a great time watching the ducks and turtles swimming around. The fee is around €3.00 per person for 20 minutes. If you rent one, make sure you get close to the gorgeous Temple of Asclepius in the middle of the lake to appreciate its stunning engravings.

Also in the park is Galleria Borgehese, a small museum that houses famous Bernini sculptures. We didn't visit because we thought it would be boring for the kids to spend two hours looking at pieces of art. However, it is certainly a highly recommended spot for adults. If you decide to go, make sure you purchase tickets ahead of time because slots are limited (see *http://www.galleriaborghese.it* for details on tickets and hours).

End your trip to Villa Borghese by visiting the Pincio Promenade, which is located in the eastern section of the park. This area features amazing sculpture busts of well-known figures, as well as a cool water clock. As you continue walking east, you'll reach a terrace with a beautiful view of the city from atop the Pincian hill, including a view of Piazza del Popolo down below.

Piazza del Popolo

What is it? Famous piazza
Address: *Piazza del Popolo, 00187 Rome, Italy*
Hours: Mon–Sun, 24 hours a day
Admission: Free
Recommended Duration: About 2 hours

From the Pincio Promenade in Villa

Borghese, walk for around ten minutes down several sets of stairs until you get to Piazza del Popolo, a wide-open oval-shaped piazza whose name translates to "Piazza of the People."

At the center of the piazza is an eye-catching Egyptian obelisk with four lion sculptures at its base.

Spend the late afternoon and early evening in this area for some awesome free entertainment for the kids. There are many street shows and music performances that make you feel alive right in the middle of the city—acrobatics, fire-shows, and mimes, to name just a few. When we visited, there was a gentleman entertaining kids with gigantic soap bubbles, which kept our girls giddy for half an hour.

There are three main streets that lead into Piazza del Popolo from the south: Via di Ripetta, Via del Corso, and Via del Babuino. They're all walk-friendly and littered with shops, gelaterias, and restaurants. This is a good time to do some light shopping if you are planning on purchasing anything in the city. We walked along Via del Corso, mainly because my wife wanted to shop at KIKO Milano (a local makeup brand). While she did that, my kids and I waited outside listening to a young lady playing her violin on the sidewalk.

Strolling around these three main streets and the Piazza del Popolo is the perfect place to experience *la passeggiata*—the Italian word used to describe a social event in the early evenings where families take to the streets. The idea behind this beautiful ritual is "to see and be seen," so the locals usually dress up for the occasion and gently stroll around as they socialize with others.

Grano frutta e farina

What is it? Small cafe/restaurant
Address: *Via della Croce 49/A, 00187 Rome, Italy*
Hours: Mon–Sun, 8:00 a.m.–10:00 p.m.
Price: Around €4.00 for a pizza slice
Recommended Duration: About 45 minutes

When you're hungry, head south on the Via del Corso, and make a left on Via della Croce to get to Grano frutta e farina, which is a small garden patio-themed restaurant.

This place sells amazing *pizza al taglio*, which is a pre-made pizza that is baked in large rectangular trays. Unlike traditional thin-crust pizza, pizza al taglio translates to "pizza by the slice." This means that you order any size piece you want, and they cut and weigh it for you on the spot. They then reheat the pizza slice for you in a piping-hot oven.

There are some marvelous and unusual combinations of pizza toppings that you can choose from. Two delicious ones I remember were the pesto and the salmon. My advice is to take advantage of the fact that slices are sold by weight and get a taste of everything. They can even cut the pizza for you into small bite-size squares to share with your partner and kids.

Venchi

What is it? Gelateria & Chocolaterie
Address: *Via della Croce, 25/26, 00187 Rome, Italy*
Hours: Sun–Thu, 10:30 a.m.–11:00 p.m. | Fri–Sat, 10:30 a.m.–12:00 a.m.
Price: €2.50/€4.50 for small/large (cone or cup)
Recommended Duration: About 30 minutes

After dinner, head over to Venchi by walking east for one minute on Via della Croce (it's on the same street as Grano frutta e farina).

Venchi is a famous Italian gourmet *chocolaterie* known for its nougatine candies that are dipped in chocolate. But they also serve some of the best gelato in Rome. Combine the best of both their worlds by trying a signature gelato flavor called "Cremino Venchi," which has a hazelnut base and is covered by a layer of their dark chocolate cream.

When you order it, the server scoops up both layers and starts folding them into each other to create a heavenly explosion of flavors. If you like the taste of Nutella chocolate spread, then I guarantee that you'll love the "Cremino Venchi" flavor. It was so good that my wife had to go back for a second serving as soon as she finished the first one.

Right around the corner from Venchi is Piazza di Spagna. So if you're up to it, head there for another visit and enjoy your gelato on the Spanish Steps as you wrap up your evening.

Sunday Morning

Spend your Sunday morning in Zone 4, which includes the Colosseum, Roman Forum, Palatine Hill, and the beautiful area of Trastevere. On this day, we left the hotel at around 8:00 a.m. and returned at around 2:00 p.m. So we spent a solid six hours in that zone, which was our longest half-day.

The Colosseum

What is it? Historic landmark/amphitheater
Address: *Piazza del Colosseo, 00184 Rome, Italy*
Hours: Mon–Sun; 8:30 a.m.–varies (closing time depends on the month, see *www.coopculture.it/en/* for more details)
Admission: €12.00 per adult; children under 18 are free (note: ticket includes admission to the Roman Forum and Palatine Hill)
Recommended Duration: About 2 hours

The Colosseum is listed as the #1 place to visit in Rome because of its rich history. This magnificent amphitheater was built 2,000 years ago and was the only form of entertainment for people in the old Roman city. It's an amazing site that you shouldn't miss.

Purchase your tickets online ahead of time from the official website at *www.coopculture.it/en/* to skip the line at the ticket booth (a €2.00 on-line reservation fee per ticket applies). You can also purchase optional upgrades such as individual guided tours or access to the underground section of the Colosseum. I skipped these upgrades because my kids weren't that into historical artifacts, and I also didn't want to be at the mercy of a guided tour schedule.

I relied more on reading to my kids ahead of time about what to expect at the Colosseum, including stories of gladiators and how they fought as part of wild animal hunts for events and games.

Avoiding the guided tour also helped us move at our own pace, including hiking up the stairs and touring the artifacts. My recommendation is to start your visit early in the morning so that you avoid the rush and the midday heat.

When you're done, head out to visit the nearby Arco di Costantino (Arch of Constantine), which is a great spot to take some pictures.

Roman Forum & Palatine Hill

What are they? Historic sites
Address: *Piazza Santa Maria Nova, 53, 00186 Rome, Italy*
Hours: Mon–Sun, 8:30 a.m.–varies (closing time depends on the month; see *www.coopculture.it/en/* for details)
Admission: €12.00 per adult; children under 18 are free (note: ticket includes admission to the Colosseum)
Recommended Duration: About 1 to 2 hours

Right next to the Colosseum are the Roman Forum and Palatine Hill, which are historic ancient sites from the early days of Rome. The ticket to the Colosseum gives you entry to both the Roman Forum and Palatine Hill, so you don't need to purchase any additional tickets.

Although both these places would be a nice continuation of your Colosseum visit, they can be brutal for kids. That's because unlike the Colosseum, the Roman Forum and Palatine Hill will need a few hours to tour, and there is very little shade to hide from the intense heat. Moreover, most kids will view these sites as just rocks. By the time we were done with the Colosseum, our kids were so bored and hungry that we barely passed through either one of these sites.

If you had to pick just one of these two, I'd recommend Palatine Hill over the Roman Forum, mainly because you can see the entire Roman Forum from the perched view of the Palatine. In other words, you'll hit two birds with one stone.

The good news is that the tickets for all three sites (Colosseum, Roman Forum, and Palatine Hill) are valid for two days in a row, so you can come back later in the afternoon (during the half-day backup period) if you decide not to do them back to back.

Impiccetta

What is it? Italian restaurant in Trastevere
Address: *Via dei Fienaroli, 7, 00153 Rome, Italy*
Hours: Tue–Sun, 12:00 p.m.–3:00 p.m. & 7:00 p.m.–11:00 p.m.
Price: Around €10.00 for a pasta entrée
Recommended Duration: Around 1 hour

After your ancient history tours, head over to have lunch at Impiccetta. Although you can walk to Impiccetta from the Roman

Forum or Palatine hill (it's a 25-minute walk), I recommend taking a cab because your kids will probably be very tired from all the walking around in the morning.

Impiccetta is a well-serviced restaurant that serves generous portions and offers a couple of local Roman dishes that you must try out.

The first is the fried zucchini, which is an appetizer that is served for free as soon as you sit down.

The second is *Cacio e Pepe*, a pasta dish which means "Cheese and Pepper." They say that you'll know how good an Italian restaurant is by tasting their Cacio e Pepe because the chefs can't really hide any mistakes inside such a simple dish: pasta, black pepper, and cheese. Impiccetta's version comes in a scrumptious cheese bowl for an extra kick.

Fiordiluna

What is it? Gelateria
Address: *Via della Lungaretta, 96, 00153 Rome, Italy*
Hours: Mon–Sun, 11:30 a.m.–12:00 a.m.
Price: €2.00/€4.00 for small/large (cone or cup)

Recommended Duration: Around 20 minutes

After lunch, grab some gelato at the nearby Fiordiluna gelateria, which is a two-minute walk away from Impicetta. Start by walking north on Via dei Fienaroli, and then make a right on Via dell'Arco di S. Calisto, which becomes Piazza di Santa Rufina. Then make another right on Via della Lungaretta, where you'll see Fiordiluna a few shops down on your left.

Fiordiluna is a tiny artisanal shop that is well-known for its authentic gelato products and methods. They use high quality ingredients, and use only in-season fruits. So you won't find strawberry gelato there during winter.

Try any of their chocolate or yogurt based flavors—you won't regret it.

Trastevere

What is it? Roman neighborhood
Address: *Piazza di Santa Maria, 00153 Rome, Italy (center of Trastevere)*
Hours: Mon–Sun, 24 hours a day
Admission: Free
Recommended Duration: About 1 hour

Trastevere is a quaint neighborhood whose name means "Across the Tiber." It is a beautiful section of Rome that is not as tourist-crazy as the other areas, and you'll get to experience genuine local scenes there. Both Impiccetta and Fiordiluna are in Trastevere, so you would have tasted some of what it has to offer.

To continue exploring, start by walking back east from Fiordiluna (on Via della Lungaretta) and then make a right on Piazza di Sant'Apollonia. The street then becomes Via del Moro, which is a beautiful narrow curved road that epitomizes the cozy feel of Trastevere. When we visited, there were a few charming shops along the way that were covered with natural grape leaves flowing all over their facades.

If you keep on walking along Via del Moro, you'll reach the Ponte Sisto Bridge, which is a lovely footbridge that overlooks the Tiber River. This makes a good spot to take a selfie picture with your kids.

After Trastevere, head back to your hotel to get some rest and freshen up.

Sunday Afternoon

Sunday afternoon was left as a backup to plan for events that were beyond our control. Had our flight been delayed on Friday, or if it had rained on Saturday, we could have used our Sunday afternoon to make up for any of that lost time.

We also wanted to allow for some flexibility in case we wanted to sleep in late one day, or spend more time in a location because we were enjoying our time.

I highly recommend you do this as well, because it'll help you enjoy your vacation and not stress out about anything you might miss. Having a backup scheduled by design becomes especially valuable if one of your kids gets sick or cranky, and you need to deviate from your plan to get them back on track.

Assuming everything goes smoothly for you, though, you'll have an entire half-day at your disposal.

You can spend it on any of the "nice-to-see" places from your earlier list or on a return trip to a zone you already visited. Some landmarks, such as the Trevi Fountain, have a totally different look and feel in the evening when the lights are on.

So what did we do?

Our kids were really tired from the Sunday morning walk, and they both took a longer-than-usual nap at the hotel. My wife and I took advantage of the downtime by starting to pack our luggage and preparing for our trip the next morning.

This gave us the freedom to pick a place where we could stay up really late without worrying about the kids getting sleepy or us falling behind on our travel preparations.

When they woke up, we decided to re-visit Piazza Navona. After reading many positive reviews about it looking so much better at night, we wanted to see for ourselves.

And the reviews were spot on. Piazza Navona at night was so different that it almost felt like we were visiting a totally new piazza. It was bustling with local artists, street performers, and painters. The projector lights shining on the three fountains and sculptures gave the whole piazza a much more royal feel.

This second visit was also more pleasurable

for us because the weather was cooler, and the performers were way better. There was so much to do and see that we decided to end our trip by staying there for the rest of the night.

For dinner, we grabbed some delicious pasta from Pasta Imperiale (address: *Via dei Coronari 160 | Via Del Boschetto 112, 00186 Rome, Italy*), a tiny shop close by that serves fresh pasta in takeaway boxes (price: around €5.00 per pasta dish).

Then we had a final round of gelato from Punto Gelato (address: *Via Dei Pettinari 43, 00186 Rome, Italy*), a gelateria popular for its sorbets (price: €2.00–5.00 per cup or cone).

Afterwards, we strolled around Piazza Navona to absorb our last experience of *la passeggiata* before heading back to the hotel and calling our vacation over.

Conclusion

We just covered a step-by-step itinerary that will help you plan for your trip with your kids.

One suggestion I have is to go back to the beginning of the book and re-read the "Three Things to Do Before Your Trip" section. This will help you plan ahead and make sure you'll get the most out of your trip.

Then, as you get closer to your date of travel, I recommend that you check any potential closing dates of the main landmarks that you'll visit. That's because some of them, such as the Spanish Steps, might be closed for planned renovations. Other landmarks might also be closed during public holidays. Knowing all that info ahead of time will help you modify your trip and avoid any potential disappointment.

Also, if you haven't done so already, make sure you download the complimentary PDF guide so you have a nice visual of the different paths you will take.

Visit the following link to download the free guide:

http://thecouchmanager.com/riwbonus

Finally, remember that FOMO (Fear of Missing Out) and FOBO (Fear of Better Options) are your enemies during your journey. The best trips are about who you're *with* and not about what you *do*. Even if things don't go 100% according to plan, don't lose focus on the big picture: you're in Rome and this is a vacation.

So enjoy it with your family.

Thank You!

I'd like to thank you once again for purchasing this book. I hope you found it helpful, and I wish you the best on your trip.

I know there are a lot of books about Rome, and the fact that you chose this one and read all the way to the end means a lot to me.

I'd like to ask you for a small favor.

If you enjoyed this book, I'd be very grateful if you leave an honest review on Amazon (I read them all).

Every review counts, and your support really does make a difference.

Thanks again for your kind support!

Cheers,

Hassan

Would you like to write a book like this one?

This is my first-ever travel book, and I wrote it while being a full-time employee, a full-time father, and a full-time procrastinator.

Writing a book is a process that's a lot easier than what most people think.

In fact, I've written three other books as a part-time author.

If you would like to write a book like this one yourself, check out my latest Amazon #1 Best Seller:

Write Your Book on the Side: How to Write and Publish Your First Nonfiction Kindle Book While Working a Full-Time Job *(Even if You Don't Have a Lot of Time and Don't Know Where to Start)*

Here's what a few people thought of it:

"As a full-time Harvard Trauma surgeon, a full-time researcher and a full-time father of 3, I do not have the time to write a book on the side. Or so I thought. This book completely challenged my misconceptions

and deeply motivated me to write a book myself."
- Dr. Haytham Kaafarani, Assistant Professor of Surgery, Harvard Medical School

"Publishing your own book will help you clarify the message you want the world to hear. This concise, smart read shows you exactly how to do it, step-by-step."
- Dave Stachowiak, Host of the "Coaching for Leaders" podcast

"Highly readable, accessible, and positive, with practical tips and a systematic framework for the writing and publishing process."
- Rob Archangel, Owner and Co-founder of "Archangel Ink"

Visit the following link to check out my "Write Your Book on the Side" book:

thecouchmanager.com/bookontheside

Made in the USA
Columbia, SC
27 September 2019